The End is Near

The END Is NEAR

Planning the Life You Want
after the Kids Are Gone

AMIE EYRE NEWHOUSE

NEW YORK

LONDON • NASHVILLE • MELBOURNE • VANCOUVER

The End is Near

Planning the Life You Want After the Kids Are Gone

© 2021 Amie Eyre Newhouse

Published in New York, New York, by Morgan James Publishing in partnership with Difference Press. Morgan James is a trademark of Morgan James, LLC. www.MorganJamesPublishing.com

ISBN 9781642798920 paperback
ISBN 9781642798937 eBook
ISBN 9781642798944 audio
Library of Congress Control Number: 2019953300

Cover Design Concept: Jennifer Stimson

Cover Design: Christopher Kirk www.GFSstudio.com

Interior Design: Chris Treccani www.3dogcreative.net

Editor: Moriah Howell

Book Coaching: The Author Incubator

Morgan James is a proud partner of Habitat for Humanity Peninsula and Greater Williamsburg. Partners in building since 2006.

Get involved today! Visit
MorganJamesPublishing.com/giving-back

For Jim, because the kitchen isn't my room.

TABLE OF CONTENTS

Chapter 1:

The End Is Near

The end is near.

What a terrible way to start a book. That first line is pretty dark! But if you're holding this book in your hands right now, you already know that the end is near. Perhaps you're dreading the looming empty nest. Maybe you have no idea what you're going to do with yourself when you – oops, I mean when your kids – grow up. Maybe you've been seeing this transition coming for a long time and you're wisely planning in advance, or maybe your youngest graduates next month and you're panicking.

Then again, you could be facing a transition that you weren't expecting whatsoever. Maybe you've experienced an illness or an injury and can no longer work in the same occupation as before. Maybe you've lost your spouse to death or divorce, and your hand has been forced – you have to find a new career in order to pay the bills. Perhaps the type of job you've been doing for your entire adult life no longer exists. Maybe you have experienced a crisis that you could only have planned for if your crystal ball was working. No matter the reason that you've bought this book, welcome.

> *"New beginnings are often disguised
> as painful endings."*
> **– Lao Tzu**

The socioeconomic role of women in American society today is drastically different than that of those who have come before us. Gone are the days of vegetable gardens, cross-stitching, bridge clubs, and quilting circles. Today we find ourselves stretched impossibly thin between our homes, our families, and our jobs. The rapidly rising cost of living has made it almost impossible for families to survive on a single income. The burden of emotional labor is largely carried by women, and mothers remain the primary parent in over half of all households. Women today are busy, stressed, and tired.

Not only are we busy, stressed, and tired, we are constantly blasted with advertising telling that we should be thinner, happier, and prettier. Oh, and younger! Somehow we are also supposed to magically avoid aging while we are exercising, eating healthy, raising our kids, working our full- time jobs, keeping the house clean, and the dog fed. We're also supposed to somehow conform to the expectations of our chosen religion and native culture while not letting any of our other womanly responsibilities slip. By the time your firstborn goes to elementary school, you have joined the ranks of overwhelmed and exhausted zombie moms.

American women become zombie-fied by the demands of motherhood. We quite literally have our brains eaten out of our heads by endless to-do lists, mountains of laundry, and conference calls. Well, maybe not our brains, but most definitely our souls. We lose track of who we are and what brings us deep joy. We forget those things that once gave purpose and meaning to our lives before we were responsible for the wants and needs of a small army of tiny humans. We become strangely myopic, focusing only on our kids' and our spouse's needs. Soccer games and T-ball practices replace our spin class and yoga practices, and nightly homework and mandatory reading overtake the time we used to spend on our hobbies or with friends. Vacations are planned around the need to give our kids "experiences" and weekends are spent shuttling kids between church services and sports practices. If you're really lucky, your kids will be super social, and you'll have other people's children to feed and supervise and entertain each weekend.

Then one day, as if overnight, our kids are gone. They go away to college and they move out. They do exactly what we always wanted them to do – they become functional adults. Ok, maybe not fully functional adults, but they do age into adulthood, nonetheless. Around the time your youngest starts driving, you find yourself increasingly panicked, wondering what in the world you are going to do with yourself when your services are no longer needed. You're finally going to have time to focus on yourself and what satisfies your soul, but there's just one teensy weensy problem: you have no idea what that is. Worse yet, you have no idea how to figure that out.

> *"I did not see any deliciousness anywhere when it came to being an adult female. I saw women who prioritized husbands and families; shopped, cooked, cleaned, drove the station wagon and made everyone else's lives run smoothly. I saw women who were self-sacrificing, who ignored their own needs, and who gave up on their own happiness. I saw women who looked hollow and dead inside; women who were bitter, hollow, resentful and resigned."*
> **– Regina Thomashauer**

The cultural and religious homogenization of the American mother is insidious and starts in childhood.

We are taught that we should look like and behave like a "lady." We are taught singularly female virtues such as modesty, submissiveness, and self-sacrifice. We are told that we are singlehandedly responsible for the happiness of our children and our spouses. We learn that our joy is solely supposed to come from seeing our children happy and our spouses successful, and that we are to deny our own desires in deference to theirs. The model woman is attractive, slender, successful at her job, beloved by her well-groomed and perfectly behaved children who always get straight As, an excellent cook and a fastidious housekeeper, and sexually and emotionally available to her spouse one hundred percent of the time. We learn that in order to be successful adult women, we have to trade our individuation for the happiness of our families.

Individuation is the developmental process of becoming oneself. According to Jungian psychology, individuation is the process of psychological integration. As stated in *Psychological Types* by C.G. Jung, "In general, it is the process by which individual beings are formed and differentiated [from other human beings]; in particular, it is the development of the psychological individual as a being distinct from the general, collective psychology." This process begins in childhood and progresses through adolescence. This is our personality, our likes and dislikes, what brings us joy, purpose, and spiritual satisfaction. This is our personal expression of gender and sexuality, how we give and receive love, and how we relate to the larger world around us. We spend our entire childhood and teenage years individuating from our parents and becoming the unique human beings that we are.

In our quest to be the amazing mothers that we all want to be, however, our individuation erodes. We are worn down by the demands of modern motherhood and we craft our lives around our children. As our children begin to leave the nest, however, our lack of individuation becomes horrifyingly apparent – what *are* we going to do with ourselves when the house is empty? Maybe we'll get a job. Ok then, what job should we get? Maybe we should go back to college for something. Sure. What for? Alright, we'll get a hobby and make money off of it. Sounds great. What hobby exactly would that be? Never mind then, we'll just volunteer somewhere. That sounds fantastic. Where will you volunteer?

Our loss of individuation prevents us from being able to answer those questions. That's why you're reading this book right now, isn't it? You're reading this book because you have no idea what to do with your life once your kids have grown up. The solution to the problem lies in resolving the disconnection from our individuated self. The solution is found using the Always Y process.

The Always Y process will give you the tools you need to plan the life you want once your kids are gone. You'll learn how to use a simple six-step practice to solve complex problems by understanding yourself. The Always Y method utilizes the English language vowels – A, E, I, O, U, and Y – as steps that move you from confusion to clarity.

The steps are:

A – Assess the Situation
E – External Preferences
I – Internal Truths
O – Oh, Heck No/Oh, Heck Yes
U – Understand
Y- *You* are always the answer!

What are you going to do with yourself once your kids are gone? Let's find out!

CHAPTER 2:

Well, That Didn't Go as Planned...

"And remember, I'm not only the Hair Club
president, but I'm also a client!"
– **Sy Sperling,** Hair Club For Men

Since you're reading this book, you're probably old enough to remember that commercial. The man with the full head of thick, luscious hair conspiratorially leans in and runs his hands through his hair to demonstrate how well the product has worked for him. It was a stroke of pure marketing genius based on human behavior: if it could work for that guy, it could work for anyone. When people ask me how I know that the Always Y method will work for them, my answer is this: I'm not only the president of the Always Y Club, I'm also a client.

Have you ever known someone who just seems to catch all the breaks? Someone who's never had a chronic or debilitating health problem; who's never been depressed, or struggled with anxiety; whose medicine cabinet holds nothing but some random band-aids and a bottle of ibuprofen? How about the person who was raised in a happy, healthy home? You know the one – the person who was raised by two loving parents, had a reasonably good relationship with their siblings and extended family, and still enjoys family gatherings to this day. We all know the woman who barely thought about getting pregnant and popped out a healthy eight-pound bundle of joy, and had a completely "natural" birth without drugs or complication, of course – and then breast fed not only that child, but also each successive one blissfully, for at least a full year. And we all know someone whose parents funded their college education, paid for a lovely wedding, gifted them the down payment for their first house, and still pays the bill when they all go out for dinner.

And how about those rags-to-riches success story people that we know? Or the ones who can eat whatever they want and still fit into their wedding dress twenty years and three kids later? Or the ones who have been happily working at the same company their entire adult life; who've paid off their first house because they never had to move across the country for a job; who are fully vested in their retirement fund, *and* get more than a two percent raise every year? How about the ones whose kids were always star athletes; who got all A's and B's without an IEP or a 504 Plan; who didn't struggle with ADD/ADHD, dyslexia or any other disability; who never got into trouble or were never seriously bullied, and who grew into attractive, stable, independent adults with seemingly little more effort on their parents' part than firm bedtimes and regular dental appointments?

None of those people are me.

I was the first-born child of a marriage that was already doomed. My father was a violent drunk and my mom was a teacher who had an adversarial relationship with her own mother. I'd tell you more about my origins, but I honestly don't know much more than that. I do hold a few tender memories of my first dog and my very own horse.

I have a younger sister just three years younger than me, but I have no memories of her until I was in third grade. I actually have very few memories at all before the age of six. The memories that I do have are not ones that I particularly care to reminisce about; I remember being locked in my bedroom at night, and I remember peeing underneath the blue rug in my room because I couldn't get out of my bedroom to use the restroom. I remember being terrified of fire, although I still have no idea why, and having horrific repetitive nightmares for years of being caught in an inferno because the door was locked. I remember lying in bed at night for hours, unable to sleep because I was locked in, obsessively listening for the sound of the fire that I was certain would consume me. I have no memories of my father outside of the night that the police came with lights a-blazing and arrested him while I hid at the neighbor's house, watching the spectacle through their dining room curtains.

Speaking of neighbors, I also remember the teenage girl from next door who babysat me in the afternoons while my mother was at work. Actually, I don't remember any details about her personally, but I remember the endless games of "doctor" that I played with her brother and the circa-1970's Fisher Price doctor kit that he used to examine me with. I was always the patient. I also clearly remember the special game of hide and seek that she and I alone would play; the one that would always end with us in her closet, naked from the waist down, doing confusing things that I wasn't supposed to tell anyone about.

My mom both found Jesus and got remarried when I was six years old. He and my mom had two daughters together, making me the oldest of four sisters. My stepfather Joe was a cruel man; also an alcoholic, he differed from my father in that he turned his rage on me and my sisters instead of my mother. He was a strict disciplinarian who took a perverse pleasure in finding new and inventive ways of causing physical pain as punishment for wrongs committed. He was an outwardly charming man, a chameleon of sorts, given to taking on different personalities depending on who he was with at the moment. Joe also had a propensity for embezzling money from his employers, which led to us moving frequently and without warning.

I was raised from that point on in a strict evangelical Christian home. My mom, desperate for happiness, gave up chain smoking and white wine for Bible reading and prayer. We went to church three times each week and hosted weekly Bible studies in our home. My sisters and I were raised to be "Proverbs 31 women," meaning that we were supposed to be able to cook, clean, raise children, earn a living, dress modestly, look appealing and be intelligent – all at the same time. The concept of the "helpmeet" was pounded into us and our roles in life were decided for us. The man was the head of the household and women were god's lesser creation, incapable of making wise decisions or fending off the wiles of temptation. As the oldest daughter, I was expected to be the junior wife to my stepfather and a second mom to my two youngest sisters. I was raised to function in the role of the helpmeet (a woman whose purpose in life is to help meet the needs of her parents and spouse) instead of being raised to simply be myself, whoever that was going to be.

Additionally, my parents assigned each of us an identity that we were expected to personify. I was the hard worker, and my sisters were given the roles of the pretty one, the smart one, and the athletic one. My worth was tied to how helpful or industrious I was at any given moment. Every aspect of our lives was planned for us in alignment with the identities we had been assigned. As the hard worker, I was indispensable at home and was not allowed to socialize, play sports, or have any extracurricular interests.

It wasn't just my internal identity that was decided for me – it was also my external identity. My mom was obsessed with being thin; she was constantly dieting, exercising, counting calories, standing on the scale and pinching her stomach in the mirror, bemoaning her imagined obesity and poor genes. My two youngest sisters, sharing the same paternal DNA, were both extremely petite in build and stature. My immediate younger sister was graced with the height, build, and features of our own father. I was not athletic or tall, and I was not a petite or unusually slender child. By default, I became the fat daughter. Along with puberty came unexpectedly large breasts and curvy hips, which only added to my self-loathing. I saw myself inextricably tied to the identity I had been given: hard working but regrettably fat. By the time I was eleven years old, I was calorie counting and dieting, hiding my breasts and hips under baggy clothes, constantly trying to reach the mythical utopia of being thin enough in my mother's eyes.

My stepfather wasn't just a violent man, he was also a pedophile, and he favored girls. An older gentleman named Bill lived with my stepfather when he and my mother got married, and Bill continued to live there until we moved away sometime later. Bill had a bedroom and bathroom of his own and he kept the door locked at all times. Bill functioned as a babysitter when my mom was at work, and Joe had an office that he worked out of there at the house. Bill, however, had an affinity for amateur photography, and Joe was happy to supply a new, live-in subject for him to photograph. I've often wondered why I have so few childhood memories, but honestly, I'm glad that I don't have any more than I do. The few memories that I do have are more than enough.

The sexual abuse continued well into my teens. There is no need to dredge through it any further except to point out how horribly contradictory the beliefs and practices regarding sexuality were in our home. One of the foundational tenets of evangelical Christianity is that sex is intended for marriage only, and we were a strict evangelical family. Purity rings and vows of celibacy until marriage were mandatory, as were one piece bathing suits and modest clothing. And yet, one my most horrifying memories is of my parents punishing me for coming home late one evening, and my stepfather angrily hissing the words, "If I can't have you, nobody can!" at me. I was seventeen years old.

I entered adulthood with my identity decided for me, my sense of self beaten out of me, my appearance pre-judged and labeled, and my sexual autonomy bulldozed. I am so grateful that I at least knew what I wanted to do with my life; I wanted to be a nurse, and that is exactly what I became. Nursing gave me the opportunity to be the hard worker that I was, but it also gave me the opportunity to be really good at something that was no one's idea but my own. I met and dated my husband Jim while in nursing school, and that time period truly was the beginning of my metamorphosis into the woman that I am today.

My identity took on another dimension when we had our kids. We struggled to have children, miscarrying two and burying one before we had our two healthy babies. My life then became consumed with being the best mom that I could possibly be for our kids, while still working as a nurse. Nursing sustained my soul in a way that nothing else could. I was very, very good at it, and I loved it. Being a nurse gave me the opportunity to develop a sense of self that I had previously not had and desperately needed. Being a mother allowed me to see the myriad of ways that my upbringing was not healthy, and I was able to grow emotionally along with our children. Over the years I began to see myself as the smart, strong, caring, spiritual person that I am.

I was completely fulfilled: I had an occupation that brought me deep joy and a sense of purpose, I had the husband of my dreams, and I was the mother for my kids that I wished that mine had been able to be for me. If you had asked me who I was, I would have answered without hesitation: wife, mom, nurse.

And then Jim found a lump in my breast.

Breast cancer. One in eight American women will be diagnosed with breast cancer during their lifetime. If you haven't done your breast self-exam recently, go do it now. If you have a family history of breast or ovarian cancer and aren't current on your mammograms, go call and make the appointment right now.

I'll wait.

The diagnosis of breast cancer was heartbreaking but not insurmountable. As a nurse, I was able to navigate through the myriad of appointments with specialists and the dizzying array of treatment choices with confidence. We decided on the double mastectomy with concurrent reconstruction which, because of the type and stage of cancer I had, allowed me to avoid chemo. I was completely at peace with our decision; I was trading my breasts for my life. We talked the kids through our decision, informed all our family and friends, made arrangements to make sure the kids got to school and church and back for a few weeks, took five weeks medical leave from my job at the hospital, and went ahead with the surgery.

Let me preface what comes next with this: I don't believe that my experience was the norm. There aren't any statistics available to verify this, but anecdotally, it appears that my journey was unusually bumpy. I have made many lifelong friends thanks to being part of the pink ribbon club, and most of them do pretty well with their reconstructive journey. If you or a loved one is considering mastectomies with reconstruction, please don't base your decision on my experience – talk to your healthcare providers and make the decision that's best for you.

My surgery went well and I returned home as planned on the fourth day. The mental transition from my original large natural breasts to the smaller reconstructed new ones was not easy, but they looked fantastic, and I was able to console myself with the fact that I would never have to wear a bra again. They sat high and tight; they certainly weren't going anywhere, and – bonus – I was able to keep my own nipples! Things didn't look like completely like "me," but being able to keep my nipples was a triumph of recent science that helped my mind adjust to the changing landscape of my own body easier. Two weeks after the initial surgery, however, my right nipple turned black, and off to the wound care center I went to try to save the nipple.

What happened after that can be summed up in one simple sentence: infection, boob out, boob in, switch sides; infection, boob out, boob in, switch sides and repeat – for a total of twelve additional surgeries. My body rejected the biological material that was used to reinforce the original reconstruction, resulting in fluid collections that became infected and caused the reconstructions to fail. It seems like an entirely different lifetime ago now, and I can tell the story with humor these days, but it was absolutely horrible. I quite literally almost died from the infections twice, my kidneys failed once, and one of the expanders tore through its support and fell about six inches down my abdominal wall. That was an adventure in and of itself: until I was healthy enough to have surgery once more, Jim and I would have to push the expander back up into the breast pocket and support it with copious amounts of medical tape so that it stayed as far north as possible each day. All in all, it took thirteen surgeries in fifteen months to put Humpty Dumpty back together again.

I ended up with a bilateral latissimus transfer reconstruction, which is (in incredibly overly simplistic terms) where they take a layer of your lat muscles from your back, unhook them from your spine, pull them around to your chest and secure them to your sternum. The muscle is then used to support the weight of an implant, and a layer of pectoral muscles are pulled over the top half of the implant to hold it in place. Thanks to the many complications and surgeries, the scars on my back seemed horrific to me. The agreement was that I would trade my breasts for my life – carving up my back like a Thanksgiving turkey wasn't part of the deal. Yet, there I was, with two jagged scars below my shoulder blades almost extending to my spine in addition to the destruction that the many infections and surgeries had wrought on my chest.

While my body image took a solid beating from the ordeal, it was my identity that took the biggest hit. One year earlier, I had ruptured a disc in my lower back, and the cumulative surgical changes in the musculature of my upper body put additional strain on it. The stress on my lower back as it compensated for the loss of strength and mobility in my upper body, combined with the stringent physical restrictions I now had to adhere to, was a killer. I was unable to run the vacuum around my bedroom, much less was I able to lift patients. I could no longer work as a bedside nurse, and I was heartbroken and lost. The identity that I had found so much joy and fulfillment embodying was gone, and once again, I had absolutely no idea who or what I was.

What was I going to do with my life now? Who was I if I wasn't a nurse? I was still a wife and mother, thank heavens, but I was acutely aware that my kids were rapidly heading towards college and independence. My husband traveled extensively for work, my kids were growing up, and I was fully and completely adrift. I felt like the body that I had always hated had turned against me and cost me the ability to do the job that gave my life purpose. Yes, there are many jobs for RNs that don't require any form of physical labor, and I had no trouble finding work, but I was no longer Amie the Nurse. I had, by necessity, become Amie, the Pusher of Desks. No more patients to care for, no more skillset to excel at, no more new nurses to mentor, and no more identity. Perhaps someone with a healthier and stronger sense of self would have been able to assimilate this change and adapt easier, but not I. I was absolutely crippled by the loss of the identity I had clung to for almost two decades.

And so began the journey to discover who I really was. Who was I when all of the identities I had been given were stripped away? Who was I now that I could no longer be the nurse that I wanted to be? Who was I going to be once my kids were gone? Over the next five years I read everything I could find that seemed like it might have the answer. I took up yoga, I became a runner, I went back to college to work on my master's degree, and I learned how to make jewelry. I was incredibly fortunate to be surrounded by a community who loved me and supported me in all my endeavors.

And then we moved across the country.

Now, not only did *I* not know who I was, absolutely no one around me knew me either. I was alone and lonely and lost. At the time I felt like I had hit absolute emotional rock bottom, and I had – but in hindsight, I am able to see that this was exactly what I needed. Without anyone around me who knew me as Amie the Nurse, I was able to construct my sense of self-worth and my identity from scratch. I took up meditation to help control my raging anxiety and started practicing mindfulness to ground myself. The concept and practice of mindfulness slowly seeped into every area of my life, and I gradually began to truly discover myself. I began to integrate mindfulness into conversations with my kids and my friends, and without realizing it, the Always Y process was born.

CHAPTER 3:

The New Vowels: A/E/I/ O/U and Always Y

Now that we understand the depth of the problem, how do we dig our way out? Let me introduce the Always Y process to you and explain how using it will change your life.

All English speakers are familiar with this little saying that helped us remember the vowels: A, E, I, O, U, and sometimes Y. We are going to give new meaning to the first five vowels, and we are going to give permanent citizenship to the letter Y. In fact, you'll learn that all of those other vowels are meaningless unless they are integrated into the letter Y! (Spoiler alert: the "Y" in this process is *you*, and you're amazing.)

After we've briefly looked at an overview of the process, we'll learn how to apply the practice of mindfulness to our exploration of the problem. As we've learned, the loss of our personal identities, or de-individualization, is the true source of the problem. You really *are* having an existential crisis – who are you outside of calendar keeper and referee? Until we've re-discovered the woman that lies under all the to-do lists and piles of laundry, we'll never be able to help her find a meaningful way to spend the next twenty years of her life. The good news is that this isn't an impossible task! As a matter of fact, you'll be surprised at how shockingly simple it really is, and better yet – you'll be amazed at the woman you'll find.

> *"I am out with lanterns, looking for myself."*
> **– Emily Dickinson**

The new vowels:
A – Assess the situation
E – External Preferences
I – Internal Truths
O – Oh, Heck No/Oh, Heck Yes
U – Understanding
Always Y – *You* are always the answer!

We're going to repurpose the letter "A" from standing for apple to "Assess the Situation." You can't solve a problem without knowing what you already have on hand. As they say, start at the very beginning, it's a very good place to start…a solid objective physical assessment is the foundation of bedside nursing care. At the beginning of each shift, the nurse will make rounds, performing a thorough physical assessment of the patient and asking key questions that yield more facts.

We find the solution to our problem by first starting with an accurate assessment of the facts. Who are you? What do you have? What do you almost have? How much do you have? How long do you have? And lastly, what do you want? These objective data give us a starting inventory by which to measure what it will take to reach our goal.

The letter "E" takes on the meaning of "External Preferences." We're going to start reacquainting ourselves with our true selves by discovering what our likes and dislikes are now. Your entire daily life has been wrapped around your family's lives for years now, as you've done everything within your power to meet their needs and to nurture them. How many years has it been since you really thought about what your favorite *anything* is? Can you even remember the last time you spent an entire twenty-four-hour period doing whatever you wanted to do? Eating whatever you wanted to eat from whatever restaurant you liked best? Sleeping and waking on a schedule designed solely around your personal needs?

What if the only person that you ever had to please ever again was yourself – what would that even look like?

The letter "I" will then stand for "Internal Truths." This is where we will learn how to hear our own individual voice again. You've grown and changed over the years: your values have shifted, even if only ever so slightly. Perhaps your spiritual beliefs have changed completely, or perhaps you hold the same beliefs more deeply. Those things that hold meaning to you now may look nothing like what was important to you years ago. If you've come to this place in life as the result of a traumatic event or life change, you may not realize exactly how deep these changes may run and how they have so beautifully impacted who you have become.

You won't have any trouble remembering what the letter "O" stands for now! O is for "Oh, Heck No/Oh, Heck Yes." Let me tell you, I may not always know what I want to do, but I can always name ten things that I sure as heck *don't* want to do!

This is the part of the process where you'll get clear on your "Hard No's" and why you want nothing to do with them. Hard No's are incredibly important, and those of us who grew up in abusive homes, have survived abusive marriages, or have spent our lives living within a culturally or religiously repressive environment have had our Hard No's chosen for us. Perhaps your Hard No has even been taken away from you by an abuser or by choices made out of desperate necessity; perhaps your Hard No's have been trampled on or stomped out by the circumstances you've lived through or the environment you've lived in. Let's take them back.

Your Hard No's have value. They have worth. Knowing your negative absolutes – those things that you will never do, those hard lines that you want never to cross – is invaluable. Whether they be many or they be just a handful, your negative absolutes give rise to your positive aspirations. You're here with me today because you don't know where you're going, and we are going to start by being very clear on where you don't want to go!

Your "Hard Yes's" are equally important as your Hard No's. You can think of a Hard Yes as the stepping stones across your muddy lawn – no matter what the rest of the landscape looks like, the stepping stones are safe places to step. You know that they are solid and firm, despite the uncertainty of the mud everywhere else. Your Hard Yes's are things that you don't have to think twice about saying yes to.

We'll use the letter "U" to represent the word "Understanding." We're going to use all of the subjective and objective data we've gathered in the previous three vowels (E, I, and O) to understand who we have become. You've grown and changed and evolved in ways that you may never have imagined and in ways that you may not even be aware of yet.

The woman you have become is a gorgeous, amazing individual, inside and out. The world needs you – not the you of twenty years ago, but the you of today. The depth of experience and wisdom you now hold is invaluable. Your viewpoint, knowledge and expertise is unique to you and is not reflected in any other woman on earth. You are no longer the chief cook and bottle washer, the calendar keeper and referee: you are a woman through whom the river of life runs deep, and you are magnificent to behold.

Lastly, the letter Y joins us here as a permanent citizen. No longer just "Sometimes Y", the letter Y has been elevated to "Always Y" status. "Y" is for You: *You* are always the answer. At this point in the process, you will once again be intimately acquainted with yourself; you will have all of the information you need to solve your problem. Once you know what materials you're working with, what you do and don't like, what does and does not hold meaning for you and what you absolutely won't do, you'll be able to decide what you truly do want to do. You are always the answer.

The beauty of the Always Y process is that it is incredibly versatile. Any kind of problem can be resolved using this method, and it can be tailored for any age group and situation. It can be used in the workplace to find common ground interpersonally, and it can be used by teens to make decisions regarding career goals and college choices; it can be used to make financial goals and create realistic household budgets. We've even used it in our family to decide how we want to spend our family vacation!

"The unexamined life is not worth living."
– Socrates

Now that we've looked at the process, let's look at how we are going to implement it.

The concept of mindfulness is loosely explained as the practice of being intentionally aware of your thoughts, feelings, sensations, and environment in the present moment. Mindfulness is taught by mental health professionals as a method of combating anxiety, quieting the fight-or-flight response, and grounding. Mindfulness is taught in the Buddhist and Hindu traditions as part of the concept of impermanence, which is that all things in the earthly realm are in a constant state of flux, and therefore nothing is permanent. Today, even large corporations are utilizing mindfulness practices to improve productivity and increase creativity among employees.

"Paying attention, on purpose, in the present moment, and non-judgmentally."
– Jon Kabat Zinn

When practicing mindfulness, external data is simply observed. No opinion is formed of the data and no decisions are made based on the data. Mindfulness takes the measurement and stops there; thoughtfulness takes the measurement and then forms an opinion of it. Mindfulness is the practice of observing a sensation or a thought without attaching meaning to it. Thoughtfulness, therefore, could be considered the opposite. Thoughtfulness receives the sensation or thought and makes a mental decision regarding it. While this may seem like an impossible distinction, it's actually quite easy once you get the hang of it.

Mindfulness exercises and meditations are generally used to bring one's awareness to the present moment. This can be done in many ways, but the difference between practicing mindfulness and just being attentive and alert is the absence of judgement. We collect external and internal data continuously, both consciously and unconsciously. Our conscious minds use this data to make judgments and form opinions, and our internal body systems use this data to adjust to our surrounding environment.

Examples of Thoughtfulness (Judgments) vs. Mindfulness (Observations)

Thoughtfulness	Mindfulness
It's hot in here	The air feels warm
It's really windy	I feel the wind
I'm hungry	My stomach is growling
My head is killing me	I have a headache
It's crowded in here	There are other people here
You make me so angry	I feel angry
You make me so happy	I feel happy
My heart is broken	I feel sad

Mindfulness Made Easy

The first time I tried to explain the practice of mindfulness to my husband, he looked at me like I was speaking a foreign language. The statement "If you can't teach it to someone else, you don't really understand it yourself" has always been a qualifier for me, both at work and as a parent, and I had obviously failed. Thankfully, my years as an elementary school nurse gave me daily opportunities to refine my skills. We are going to use the same practice of mindfulness that helps five-year-olds with separation anxiety calm themselves to rediscover ourselves.

Read the following paragraph through once for understanding and then a second time to take a moment to process each statement. This is an easy guided meditation useful for centering oneself and for calming anxiety. Remember – if your mind wanders, simply bring it back to the present. The only way to do mindfulness "wrong" is to not do it at all!

Sit quietly with your eyes closed for a few moments, settling yourself comfortably into your chair. Bring your attention to your breath. Notice how fast or how slow you are breathing right now. Take a slow, deep breath in, and then release it slowly and evenly. If you are able to, slow your breathing down and repeat. Do this several times until you feel like you have reached a comfortable pace. Think about the air as you breathe it in: is the air cold in your nose? Does it feel humid, or is it dry? Now think about your heart – can you feel your heartbeat as you slowly inhale and exhale? Is your heart beating slowly? If you breathe slower and more deeply, does your heartbeat slow down? Now bring your attention back to your breath, and as you take your next breath, breathe the air all the way down into your toes. Notice how your feet feel, and if they are at all uncomfortable, reposition them. Continuing to breathe slowly, mentally bring your attention slowly up from your toes into your legs. Reposition your legs if you need to, and then refocus on your breathing for a few breaths. Now notice how the chair feels underneath you: notice the temperature of the chair, the softness or hardness of it, and reposition yourself as necessary. Bring your attention up to your belly, and notice how it moves in conjunction with your breathing. Move your attention higher, noting your chest rising and falling, and pause at your shoulders. Continuing to breathe slowly and deeply, notice how your shoulders feel. Are they tense? Release any tension in your shoulders, and breathe deeply into them once more. Now notice your neck, and up further into your jaw – are they relaxed? Are you holding tension in your jaw or neck? If so, release the tension. Move your attention now up to your ears; how do they feel? Now consider the sounds that you hear. Without changing the pace of your breathing, observe the noises around you. Simply observe the sounds as they happen – don't identify them or form an opinion of them. If you find that your mind wanders to the source of the sound, simply bring your thoughts back to your breath for a few moments. Bring your attention now to your nose and the air moving through it: observe any smells and the temperature of the air. Follow a breath as you draw it into your lungs; exhale slowly, and draw another breath all the way down your arms this time into your hands. Without moving your hands, notice what they feel, and how they feel. On your next breath, bring your attention back up from your hands into your chest, and refocus on your breath. Continue breathing until you feel ready to open your eyes. Once you have opened your eyes, gently roll your shoulders and your neck, wiggle your fingers and toes, and then continue on with your day.

How to Use This Book

We'll be using this basic practice of mindfulness to get reacquainted with ourselves as we move through the Always Y process. There are "thought exercises" throughout the book designed to help you learn more about yourself. If you're someone who journals, make time for yourself to incorporate these exercises into your journaling practice. Maybe you keep notes in your phone or think best when you are typing – that's perfect. Jot your thoughts directly in the margins if that is most convenient. Maybe writing and typing aren't your thing, and you'd rather think deep thoughts while you walk your dog or use the thought exercises as meditations – those are perfect options too!

Each thought exercise is meant to be completed as though you were doing a meditation like the one above. Start by drawing your attention to your breath and centering yourself first, then consider the exercise. As you work through the exercise, do so without opinion or judgement of your responses: simply observe them. Observe and record your responses just as they come: don't judge them, filter them or form an opinion of them.

There is no wrong way to work through the thought exercises as long as you are practicing mindfulness when you do so. The thought exercises in this book have only two imperatives:

1. **Complete each thought exercise as an exercise in mindfulness.**

    Allow yourself to "free think." Note each thought as it comes without judgement or opinion. There is neither a wrong or a right answer nor a bad or a good answer. Simply register the thought and let it pass through. Your mind may wander from the topic at hand – that's completely normal and not a big deal. When that happens (and it will), just bring your thoughts back to concept at hand and continue on. If you find yourself mentally reviewing the grocery list three minutes into the exercise, don't worry about it! When you realize that your mind has wandered, simply go back to the thought exercise until you are done.

2. **Record your observations for each exercise.**

   This is important. Write down a few short phrases or single word observations after each exercise, keeping track of which step they belong under. Even if you are working through the thought exercises in the form of journaling or typing notes, you'll want to write down a few short phrases or single word observations after each step. These words, phrases and conclusions are the gold you will be mining later on in the process as you design the next phase of your life.

Some of the thought exercises will be easier for you than others. This is completely normal! The important thing is to stick with it. Repeat the exercise ten times if you have to. Investigate each concept as though you were getting to know someone that you care deeply about – because you are. You are getting to know *yourself*. You are not the same woman you were when you were eighteen years old, trying to grow up as fast as possible. You've grown and changed; you've experienced great joys and deep pains; you've learned new skills and forgotten old ones; you've discovered new interests and left old ones behind. The young woman who may have once felt like the world is her oyster may no longer even like shellfish. Let's find out what she *does* like!

CHAPTER 4:

Assess the Situation

Solving problems are similar to cooking: you need to know what ingredients you have on hand before you can even start. Imagine that you're supposed to bring a dessert to work tomorrow, so you set out to bake something (out of a box, of course, because who in the world has time to make things from scratch?!). You've got a box of brownie mix and a box of angel food cake mix. Brownies are easier to make than angel food cake, you reason logically, and set out to make the brownies. Seriously, getting an angel food cake out of an cake pan without tearing it to shreds is harder than peeling a two-year-old with separation anxiety off of you so that you can get out the door on time.

You tear open the box of brownies, dump the dry mix into the bowl, and pour the half cup of oil on top. Then you grab the eggs out of the fridge…

oh, wait – you're completely out of eggs! We've all felt the horror of getting halfway through a brownie recipe before realizing that we're completely out of eggs. Now you've got to run to the store and buy eggs before you can finish mixing them, much less bake them. If you had only looked to see what ingredients you had on hand first, you would have known that you were out of eggs, and you could have gone with the angel food cake instead. The only ingredient a box of angel food cake mix needs is water.

We're going to make a thorough list of what ingredients we already have on hand before we decide which dessert to bake.

Just the Facts, Ma'am

Assess the situation. Here you're going to gather data in order to make an informed decision. This means that you are going to take a detailed, objective assessment of everything and anything pertinent to the problem you need to solve. This is the equivalent of taking stock of what ingredients you have on hand before you choose a recipe. So many times we make decisions that we later regret because we didn't take the time to make sure we had all of the information first (eggless brownies, anyone?). Doing a thorough assessment on the front end will save you time, money, and heartache on the backend.

It's important to keep in mind that this is not supposed to be a *wish* list. This is a factual and binary accounting of your current resources, assets, and obstacles. Think of it as a personal inventory of yourself, just as you are, right now. This list might change between now and the end of the book – and that's ok. Life happens. If any of these answers change while you are working through the process, just amend your list. The key here is that this list should be factual, objective, and accurate.

Depending on your life stage and the dynamics of your household, you may not be familiar with each item on this list. There are many things that influence how much of this information you know, such as age, culture, religious practices, and marital/relationship status. You owe it to yourself to take the time to investigate any of the answers that you aren't certain of and to ask questions when needed. If you are a member of a culture or a religion where women are not allowed have access to some of the items below, simply leave those items blank for now. This is simply a fact-finding mission.

Facts + Feelings = Reaction

> *"It's rarely the facts that matter – it's the feelings around the facts that determine our reaction."*
> **– Esther Perel**

Before you delve in to this fact-finding mission, let's talk about how our psyche processes facts. As stated before, facts are simply objective pieces of data. As the inimitable Belgian couples counselor Dr. Esther Perel states so succinctly, "It's our feelings around the facts that determine our reaction." It is highly likely, therefore, that along your fact-finding journey you will be waylaid by some unexpectedly strong feelings at least once.

Why is this? Simply put, it's because you're human. All of the items in the list below carry with them the baggage of your childhood and your adulthood as experienced thus far, starting with the very first category, "*What am I?*". A question as seemingly mundane as your marital status can be difficult to answer if the factual response elicits an emotional reaction. Sometimes these emotional reactions catch us by surprise and can be incredibly overwhelming. Our emotions can then trigger our fight-or-flight response, which can in turn manifest in the form of anxiety, anger, or even the inability to finish the exercise.

Our brains are designed to absorb data and produce responses. One of the ways that our brain responds to external stimuli (data) is by eliciting an emotion. For instance, seeing an unfamiliar growling dog running towards you with its teeth bared might elicit a feeling of fear. You might feel happy upon learning that your favorite nephew is coming to visit; you might feel angry when you see muddy footprints on your freshly cleaned floor, or you might feel sad when your favorite necklace breaks. In the same way, you may experience a strong emotional response to one or more of the items below.

Be gentle with yourself. The point of this assessment is to gather factual information, not to shine a light on everything that triggers you. You don't have to do this exercise alone. Feel free to ask someone you trust to help you complete your personal inventory. In fact, if you already know that there questions on that list that will be painful for you to answer, I strongly encourage you *not* to work on this alone. Ask a trusted friend, sibling or significant other to fill it out with you. Let them complete all of the items that they know might be painful or difficult for you. You can then either finish your personal inventory yourself or have that person ask you the questions and record your answers on your behalf. The goal here is simply to build a foundation of facts upon which your solution can be built.

"Our heart, the record keeper of feelings, emotions and attachments, honors conceptions that the lucid mind might not agree with."
– Philip Larkin

◇◇◇

Thought Exercise:
Create an Objective Personal Inventory

Be As Specific As Possible

What am I?
1. Age_____

2. Gender _____

3. Marital status _____

Overall health status (list any health issues,
   injuries or disabilities that affect your daily life)

   _____

   _____

   _____

   _____

4. Physical capability (can you lift over twenty
   pounds, do you have full use of all extremities,
   etc.)

   _____

   _____

   _____

   _____

What do I have?

1. Education _____

   _____

   _____

   _____

2. Certifications _____

   _____

   _____

   _____

3. Special skills _____

   _____

   _____

   _____

4. Talents _____

   _____

   _____

   _____

5. What work experience do you have? _____

   _____

   _____

   _____

6. What unusual life experience(s) have you had?

   _____

_____
_____
_____

What do I almost have?

Unfinished college degrees?

_____
_____
_____

1. Unfinished certifications/licenses?

    _____
    _____
    _____

2. Skills or trades partially mastered?

    _____
    _____
    _____

3. Investments/pensions etc. not fully vested?

    _____
    _____
    _____
    _____

How long would it take?

1. Degree _____

_____

_____

_____

2. Certifications/licenses __ _____

_____

_____

_____

3. Skills/trades _____

_____

_____

_____

4. Investments_____

_____

_____

_____

How much do I have (financial resources)?

1. Current income (yours) _____

_____

_____

_____

2. Additional household income that you can draw from (spouse, significant other, etc.)

   _____

   _____

   _____

   _____

3. Retirement funds (the answers to this will significantly impact your goals, so you will need to know the answers to the following questions:

   A. Do I/we have sufficient retirement funds right now? _____

   B. Do I need to add to my/our retirement fund? _____

4. Am I living paycheck to paycheck or will my future income be expendable?

   _____

5. Do I need to bring in an income in the future?

   _____

6. How much debt am I responsible for (student loans, mortgage, car payments, etc.)?

   _____

   _____

_____

_____

7. What is my monthly cost of living?

_____

_____

_____

_____

What is my timeline?

1. Is there a hard deadline? If so, when?

_____

2. Is the target date for the resolution of the problem? _____

3. How much time do I have to between now and the deadline/target date?

_____

What do I want?

1. List any predetermined personal goals

_____

_____

_____

_____

2. List any predetermined financial goals

   _____

   _____

   _____

   _____

CHAPTER 5

External Preferences

Once upon a time, in a land far, far away, you were girl of hopes, dreams, desires, and pleasures. When you wanted chocolate ice cream, you ordered chocolate ice cream; when you wanted your steak cooked medium rare, you asked for your steak to be cooked medium rare; when you wanted to sleep in on a Saturday morning, you slept in. You ate the foods that you wanted to eat and you slept in on weekends without a second thought. It would never have occurred to you that you would find yourself here one day: ordering vanilla ice cream because it doesn't stain, and having your steak cooked medium well because "meat juice is gross – ew." Never in a million years would you have imagined that you would be awake at five a.m. on a Saturday because someone else wasn't tired anymore. Ah, the glory days of autonomy – where did they go?

I'll wager a guess: they went the way of two-door cars, white blouses and stiletto heels. If you're lucky, your autonomy survived the early years of cohabitation with your significant other, only to be completely absorbed by the blessed black hole of motherhood. Maybe your individuation began to unravel upon saying your wedding vows. Worse yet, perhaps the environment you were raised in prevented you from ever achieving individuation in the first place. No matter the cause, you are here now, holding this book in your hands, feeling the universe tug at your heart, calling you back to yourself.

Thought Exercise:

Grab a pen and paper and make a list of between five and ten practical, specific changes you made to your life as a result of becoming a parent (i.e. changes to your sleep schedule, foods you cook, clothes you wear, car you drive, etc.). Now go back over your list, considering whether or not each item still serves you and/or is still necessary now that your kids have grown. Circle the items that are no longer serving you and/or that are no longer necessary to continue. What can you do differently? How can your life more accurately reflect your own preferences?

_____

_____

_____

_____

_____

_____

_____

_____

_____

_____

_____

Straight lines + Sailors = Sanity

You're not the only woman who has lost track of herself while raising her family, and you aren't broken, although you may feel like both of those statements are true. You have done exactly what you have needed to do to be the mother you wanted to be for your children.

You most certainly aren't alone – just look around you the next time you are at the grocery store. See all those women with packages of frozen dinosaur shaped chicken nuggets and boxes of rainbow flavored breakfast cereal in their carts? Stop one of them, and ask her to show you five food items in her cart that she bought solely for _herself_ – items that she plans to share with another adult do not count. If she looks at you like you've asked her to recite the _Gettysburg Address,_ you've got your answer.

Now, look for a woman in the checkout line with a shopping cart full of granola bars, oranges, and seemingly hundreds of mini bottles of sports drinks. Cautiously approach her and ask her when the last time was that she slept in past nine a.m. on a weekend. If you're feeling particularly brave, ask her when the last time was that she slept completely naked – and she woke up still naked the next morning – or at least when the last time was that she slept all night in actual lingerie.

There's an old saying that we're all familiar with: "The shortest distance between two points is a straight line." Being a parent is a constant search for the straight line in life: how do we get from point A to point B as efficiently as possible? How can I get everyone out the door on time for school – without getting up at 4am? How can I feed the whole family dinner – without cooking three separate meals? How can I get eight hours of uninterrupted sleep – without drugging my kids? As a parent, our sanity rests precariously on that proverbial straight line. Our pursuit of efficiency, however, means eliminating things along the way, not unlike the clipper ships of old, dropping weight in order to gain speed.

We've all seen enough pirate movies to understand the concept of dropping weight. We know the drill: the enemy ship is rapidly approaching because the good guys just can't get moving fast enough. However will they escape this great danger? By dropping weight, of course. The captain gives the order for his crew of salty sailors to "drop weight," and all manner of heavy objects get tossed overboard. Suddenly, stripped of all its non-essential cargo, their ship surges ahead to safety, and the day is saved. Hurrah!

"Survival mode is supposed to be a phase that helps save your life. It is not meant to be how you live."
– Michele Rosenthal

So what do the proverbial straight line and the practice of dropping weight have to do with your loss of individuation? Absolutely everything, as they are the keys to surviving motherhood. Think back to the very first time you tried to leave the house with an infant. You started with a huge pile of must-have items for the baby, an empty diaper bag and your purse. You quickly realize that all of those must-have items are not going to fit in the diaper bag, so you start eliminating things. You finally whittle the pile of baby items down to what you are certain are the absolute bare essentials, put the infant in the carrier, and grab both bags to leave.

You've got the infant carrier with the sleeping baby in it hooked on one forearm and the two bags slung over your shoulder. As you try to open the door to leave, one (or both) of the bags slides forward and down your arm. If you're as lucky as I am, whichever bag that fell forward lands in the infant carrier with the baby, startling them awake. Now you're a big tangled mess of infant carrier and bag straps – with the added joy of a wailing infant. Oh, and you're probably already running late, because getting out of the house with an infant the first time is an Olympic event.

So there you are: late, frustrated, and sleep deprived, with the unpleasant bonus of a now-wailing infant. You can't leave the heavy infant carrier with the wailing baby behind (although you might have already secretly considered that), but obviously carrying both bags along with it isn't going to work. It occurs to you that perhaps you don't need to carry a separate purse after all, and you set about to put the contents of your purse into the diaper bag. But wait, there's not enough room for all of your personal items and all of the baby's items to fit in the diaper bag! And so, like our salty sailors, you begin to drop weight.

We all know how this story ends. It's not baby items that get eliminated, it's *your* personal items. Makeup bag? Gone. Cute little purse? Never to be seen again. You jam your wallet, cell phone and a lip gloss into the diaper bag and head out to the car. While this is all perfectly innocuous in and of itself, it is the harbinger of things to come. In your quest for efficiency (AKA, sanity), you will drop weight many, many more times along your parenting journey. Each time, the items deemed to be non-essential are not the children's but yours.

For many women, this relegation of their personal items as "non-essential" begins to be reflective of their preferences and desires. Like the metaphorical frog in the pot of water, it happens slowly and insidiously. The wailing infant grows to be a precocious preschooler with particular food preferences, and for the sake of efficiency (sanity), meals are now planned around what the child will eat. The advent of a sibling with a food allergy further narrows your repertoire of meals, and you begin choosing restaurants based on the contents of their kids' menu. Kids' sports, dance lessons, and play dates begin to absorb all of your weekends and evenings, and your weekly happy hour with the girls turns into Happy Meals between soccer practices. The running shoes that you used to replace every six months become three different pairs of cleats for three different sports. In our quest to be the mother that we want to be for our children, we regularly choose their needs and wants over ours.

This is not to say that we are wrong for doing so – on the contrary, the tiny humans we bring into this world rely on us to meet all of their needs, frequently at the expense of our own. The challenge, as women, is to do this without losing ourselves completely in the process. Our commercial culture complicates this further by merging the world of mother and child for profit: mommy & me yoga classes, mommy &

me clothing, mommy & me mani/pedi's. Even the clothes we wear and our few precious minutes of free time become child-centric, and our individuation erodes even further.

Thought Exercise:

Imagine what the perfect work environment would look like for you. Set a timer for two minutes and close your eyes: imagine that you are in the middle of that imaginary perfect workspace. What does it look like? What does it sound like? Fill in the details of this environment just as you would if you were physically situated in the middle of it practicing mindfulness.

_____

_____

_____

_____

_____

_____

_____

_____

_____

_____

What's Your Pleasure?

"When she ignores her pleasure, a woman can mistake her purpose and believe that her function is to enslave herself to her job or to serve her husband, her kids or her family."
– Regina Thomashauer

You've spent years learning the nuanced tastes of your children – it's time to reacquaint yourself with your own. The following thought exercises will help you redefine your likes and dislikes. Gone are the days of eating macaroni & cheese and bites of cold hot dogs off of your kids' plates in lieu of cooking one more thing… so what would you like to eat instead?

Approach these thought exercises not as "either/or" questions, but as an invitation to get to know yourself once more. If one were to think of the Always Y process as a relationship, this would be the first date. Ask yourself each question just as you would ask someone you were dating; start with a "what" question, and follow up with a "why" response. If you get stuck, it may help you to use the same technique as you would use to get your teenagers to tell you about their day at school. Remember what it was like to get them to talk about their day? Maybe your kids were more forthcoming than mine were, but the question "how was your day?" was always answered the same exact way: "fine." I would then ask them to tell me about one positive thing that happened during their day and one negative thing, and one of those would spark an actual conversation. Do the same for yourself if you don't know how to start.

Use what you've learned about the practice of mindfulness to explore each exercise thoroughly. Instead of focusing your attention on observing the present moment, however, you'll be observing your own thoughts without judgement. Consider each word or concept and simply note your reactions to it as they come. If you find yourself censoring your thoughts instead of simply observing them, just bring your attention back to the concept at hand and continue on.

Here are some examples of ways you might do this:

- *Meditation*: Set a timer for two minutes. Think about the first concept in the pair of words: define it in your own words, and then observe your thoughts and opinions as they come. Once the timer goes off, move on to the second concept, set the timer for another two minutes, and repeat the process. When the time goes off this time, set it for another two minutes; this time considering the two concepts together as a unit.
- *Free-write*: Grab a pen and paper. Fold the paper into equal thirds or draw lines to divide

it. Write the first concept down on one section of the paper. Set a timer for two minutes. Define the concept for yourself mentally and then begin to free-write. Write down any words or phrases that come to mind as soon as they appear – don't filter your responses, and don't worry about spelling or anything else. When the timer goes off, write the second concept down in another unused third and repeat the process. When the timer dings, reset it for another two minutes. This time, write both concepts in the last section, and consider them as a unit. Write your thoughts just as they come to mind – no filtering or editing.

- *Non-dominant hand free-write*: Follow the instructions above as though you were going to do a traditional free-writing exercise, but this time, write with your non-dominant hand. By switching hands from your dominant hand to non-dominant hand, you access a different part of the brain. This gives you the opportunity to explore thoughts and feelings about the concept that you may not consciously be aware of.

Important: Remember to take a few minutes after each you've finished each exercise to write down your actual preference and a few key reasons why you chose it.

Thought Exercise:
Either/Or

1. Early bird or a night owl?

   _____

2. Sweet or Spicy?

   _____

3. Physical or cerebral activities?

   _____

4. Introverted or extroverted?

   _____

5. Outside or inside?

   _____

6. Hot or cold?

   _____

7. Kids or animals?

   _____

8.   Work alone or in a group?

     _____

9.   Travel abroad or domestically?

     _____

10. Spend or save?

     _____

CHAPTER 6:

Internal Truths

When your values are clear to you,
making decisions becomes easier."
– Roy E. Disney

As we move through the years, our values and priorities evolve and change. Many of us start out our adult lives with very rigid and specific belief systems only to have them shattered – or, at the very least, permanently altered by our life experiences. Sometimes this happens in response to a specific event, and sometimes we change our views gradually over time. We may find our foundational beliefs regarding gender roles evolve as we create a family; we may experience a traumatic event that radically changes our political and/or world view; we may realize that our spiritual practices no longer resonate with us; or we may wake up one day and realize that we no longer find purpose in the pursuit of a particular career goal. Just as our bodies change with the years, so do our internal truths.

Your internal truths are the basis upon which all of your decisions are made, whether you are aware of it at the time or not. Our behavior is based on our internal truths, which are beliefs that determine our personal values and heavily influence our actions. We develop our conscious and unconscious belief systems beginning with the lessons we are taught very early in childhood and they evolve as we accumulate life experience. The environment we are raised in strongly influences the home we create for our own family, and the behaviors we saw modeled by the adults that raised us become the blueprint for how we do (or, just as frequently, how we *don't*) raise our own children.

Our internal truths are the framework for the life we live. They give shape to not only our spiritual practices but also how we move through our daily life. As you are considering what will bring purpose and fulfillment to your life once your kids are grown and gone, conscious familiarity with your internal truths will lend clarity to your decision-making process. Some values are more obvious in how they affect our lives than others: for example, someone who follows a vegan diet would not find fulfillment working in a butcher shop. However, our less obvious, even unconscious values can be just as important to consider. We may refuse to shop at a particular store because they sell items that we find offensive, we might choose our physician based on their native language, or we may not eat at a certain restaurant because we disagree with their political stance. Just as these internal truths shape the path of your daily life, they need to be taken into consideration when planning your future.

Thought Exercise:

What did you imagine you would be like at this age when you were just twenty-one years old? In what ways do you resemble that? In what ways are you different?

_____

_____

_____

_____

_____

_____

_____

_____

_____
_____

"We cannot teach the larger culture to cherish us
until we cherish ourselves."
– Regina Thomashauer

The gradual change in my own internal truth over the years is responsible for the existence of this very book. Raised to believe that a woman's role in life was to be that of the first mate to her husband's role as captain, I entered my twenties vehemently anti-feminist and a staunch conservative. I was convinced by the churches we attended and the discussions at my dinner table that women had all of the rights that they needed and that feminism was akin to atheism. Little did I know when I hit the hospital floor as a new nurse at the ripe old age of twenty-one, that the flaws in those beliefs were about to be illustrated for me time after time after time. My internal truth was about to be tested.

By the time I had turned twenty-two years old, I had been handed hundreds of Styrofoam cups by male doctors and told how many sugars they wanted in their coffee. By the time I turned twenty-five years old, an office chair had been thrown at me by an angry physician – and *I* was given a stern talking to for somehow making him angry enough to throw said chair. By the time I turned thirty, I had been repeatedly snubbed by physicians who assumed that my male nurse aide was the Charge Nurse instead of me. By the time I was thirty-five, I was painfully aware that the male nurses that worked under me were being paid significantly more than me. By the time I was forty, I had been asked, "Where is the man that you work for?" enough times to have my response to that insanity actually memorized. While nothing fazed me anymore, my beliefs about women's rights had done a full one-eighty.

The woman I am today is more a product of my life experiences than of my upbringing. The young college educated mom who had to pawn her jewelry to buy diapers has become the woman who understands that poverty is not synonymous with laziness. The middle class daughter whose mother escaped a locked dementia unit in Oklahoma and hitch-hiked to Chicago is now the woman understands that homelessness is not a character flaw. The patriotic former sister-in-law of an illegal alien is now the woman who understands that immigrants aren't the enemy. The white aunt with mixed race nieces and nephews is now the woman who understands that systemic racism is deadly. All of those women are me. My internal truths have evolved – and I am a better woman for it.

◇◇◇◇

Thought Exercise:

What strongly held values were you raised with that you no longer agree with? Why? What do you believe instead?

_____

_____

_____

_____

_____

_____

_____

_____

_____

_____

"When someone asks me what sparked my spiritual awakening: Now this is a story, all about how, my life got flipped, turned upside down..."
– Elephant Journal

Our internal truths include our spiritual beliefs and practices, no matter what they are, no matter who or what you do or don't believe in. Our spiritual beliefs manifest themselves in every area of our life: how we behave, what we do with our finances, what we eat, who we marry...everything. You may think that you know exactly what you believe, but do you really? Do you know what you *actually* believe, or is it that you know what you are supposed to believe? While those questions may seem out of place in a book about empty nesting, they are integral to understanding what will satisfy your soul in the coming years. Our spiritual beliefs directly influence our values, our values determine our behavior, and behavior defines culture.

American culture is largely based on historically Judeo-Christian values: hard work, nuclear families with a patriarchal structure, structured gender roles, financial independence, and personal responsibility. These concepts are mirrored in all Abrahamic religions with slight variations in application. In addition to those basic tenets, we hold material wealth to be both the measurement of success and the stepping stone to power. The advent of social media has given our culture an endless supply of propaganda reinforcing the wealth-and-beauty-equal-happiness myth. Our children are indoctrinated into the pursuit of material wealth and physical beauty through television and movies, and consumerism is firmly entrenched in their young minds by the appropriation of holidays as retail milestones.

Our religious beliefs regarding the pursuit of wealth and materialism clearly influence the type of career we choose, how we manage our finances and how we measure success. They also influence the type of work environment we do or don't want to work in and who we feel comfortable working for. This can be as broad as whether we work at a non-profit or a for-profit organization or as specific as choosing an employer based on whether or not they are open on Sundays. Beyond the choice of career and employer, however, our spiritual beliefs influence how we interact with those around us at work.

Thought Exercise:

Think of a specific spiritual belief that has evolved for you while raising your kids. How has the change in what you believe affected your daily life? How has it affected your values?

_____

_____

_____

_____

_____

_____

_____

_____

_____

_____

My spiritual beliefs began to change in my early twenties, yet it wasn't until I was in my late thirties that I realized how different they had become. For example, my conservative evangelical background imbued me with the belief that homosexuality was a horrible sin, and that anyone who was not heterosexually monogamous was both risking – and deserving of – the wrath of God. I didn't know anyone that was gay or lesbian when I was growing up; or if I did, they certainly weren't out of the closet. My work as a nurse, however, gave me the opportunity to both work with and care for people of all sexual orientations. It was much easier to believe that homosexuals were deserving of the horror of AIDS before I cared for countless men as they died of it. It was much easier to believe that same-sex marriage was a societal perversion before I worked alongside gay and lesbian nurses raising beautiful, healthy, happy families. It was much easier to believe that homosexuality was deviant and sinful before some of the most ethical and compassionate nurses I had ever had the honor of working alongside of were gay.

I privately disagreed with my religion's stance against homosexuality for years, teaching my children instead that God was more concerned with the contents of their heart than their preference in genitals. We continued to attend conservative churches and to shamefully pay lip service to their passionately hateful treatment of non-heterosexuals until the 2006 Texas gubernatorial race. During a televised debate between the candidates, Kinky Friedman was asked to state his position on gay marriage. His response was simultaneously simple and profound, and was the last nail in the coffin of my tolerance for homophobia.

> *"I support gay marriage. I think they have a right to be as miserable as the rest of us."*
> **– Kinky Friedman**

This is but one of my many spiritual beliefs that evolved as I raised my children, yet the effect has been wide reaching.

Thought Exercise:
Values Comparison

Suggestions for how to do the following thought exercise:

- *Meditation*: Set a timer for two minutes. Think about the first concept in the pair: define it in your own words, and then observe your thoughts and opinions as they come. Once the timer goes off, move on to the second concept, set the timer for another two minutes, and repeat the process. When the timer goes off this time, set it for another two minutes; this time considering the two concepts together as a unit.

- *Free-write*: Grab a pen and paper. Fold the paper into equal thirds or draw lines to divide it. Write the first concept down on one section of the paper. Set a timer for two minutes. Define the concept for yourself mentally and then begin to free-write. Write down any words or phrases that come to mind as soon as they appear – don't filter your responses, and don't worry about spelling or anything else. When the timer goes off, write the second concept down in another unused third and repeat the process. When the timer dings, reset it for another two minutes. This time, write both concepts in the last section, and consider them as a unit. Write your thoughts just as they come to mind – no filtering or editing.

- *Non-dominant hand free-write*: Follow the instructions above as though you were going to do a traditional free-writing exercise, but this time, write with your non-dominant hand. By switching hands from your dominant hand to non-dominant hand, you access a different part of the brain. This gives you the opportunity to explore thoughts and feelings about the concept that you may not consciously be aware of.

Important: Remember to take a few minutes after each you've finished each exercise to write down your actual preference and a few key reasons why you chose it.

Which is more...

1. Admirable: to be teachable or to be able to teach? _____

2. Enviable: spiritual depth or material wealth?

   _____

3. Valuable: life experience or higher education?

   _____

4. Inspiring: independence or community?

   _____

5. Rewarding: being productive or serving a purpose?

   _____

6. Tolerable: persistent high stress or frequent boredom?

   _____

7. Motivating: money or recognition?

   _____

8. Desirable: respect or authority?

   _____

9. Satisfying: perfection or mastery?

   _____

10. Important: career success or happiness?

    _____

Midlife Crisis or Empty Nest Syndrome?

"People may call what happens at midlife 'a crisis', but it's not. It's an unraveling – a time when you feel a desperate pull to live the life you want to live, not the one you're 'supposed' to live."
– Brené Brown

There is a very good chance that you are either already in midlife, or right on the cusp of it, given the fact that you're reading a book about empty nesting. If so, you are about to enter the Crisis Danger Zone. People generally associate the phrase "midlife crisis" with balding men, sports cars and motorcycles. Women have not traditionally been thought of as having midlife crises – instead, we are the lucky recipients of the moniker "empty nest syndrome."

We all know of a woman whose kids went off to college and then she either had an affair or her marriage imploded into divorce. I used to wonder why that seemed to happen so often when I was younger. While I am by no means an expert of any sort, my own journey through my forties has made one thing crystal clear to me: everything changes. Or perhaps I should say this instead: everything *can* change. This is part of what has drawn you to this book- you feel the changes inside of you, even if you can't name them or you don't understand them.

The phrase Empty Nest Syndrome is commonly used to refer to the overwhelming grief that some parents experience when their children leave home for college. There is no doubt that there is a period of grieving when your kids move out, but I have always suspected that there was more to the story. We are very much aware that our kids are going to leave, and as they move through their high school years and begin to drive, we see less and less of them. It's no surprise to anyone when their recently graduated high school senior goes off to college. Nature has graciously designed the teen years to be a slow and gradual weaning period for parents in preparation for the inevitable. It seems illogical that a woman who has gone through the natural progression of the child rearing process would be struck with debilitating grief when she has been knowingly working towards this inevitability for almost two decades.

My suspicion is that this is less about the kids leaving and more about the loss of personal identity.

CHAPTER 7:

Oh, Heck No/Oh, Heck Yes

Hard No's: we all have them, whether we're consciously aware of them or not. The phrase "Hard No" is used in conversation to mean "absolutely or definitely no." It's used to indicate an emphatically negative response or that the concept in question is completely unacceptable. A Hard No is an absolutely non-negotiable, no-way-in-heck-is-that-ever-happening sort of "no." A Hard No is not up for discussion, and it should be respected at all times. A Hard No also be used to signify that something is against the rules, unlawful or unacceptable. It can also be used to denote a firm personal boundary or that something is off limits.

Our Hard No's can tell us a lot about ourselves. We don't always get to choose our Hard No's, however, as many of them have been dictated to us by our culture and/or our religion. Beyond that, we often have a perhaps unconscious list of Hard No's that we respect on behalf of our parents or spouse. As our children age, they also begin to develop their own Hard No's, and we integrate and respect those too. Every job has its own litany of Hard No's; every organization has its own; every religion has its own; and every family has its own.

No Offense to Me, but *What* Am I Doing?

My hair is an example of a Hard No that was not my own. I always had long hair as a little girl. I desperately wanted to have short hair but I was not allowed to: it was a Hard No in my parent's opinion for me to have short hair. I was absolutely forbidden to have the length cut any shorter than my bra line while I lived in my parent's home. There was no religious meaning behind it; it was simply a rule because my parents both believed that short hair was not feminine. This Hard No unconsciously became my own as I grew up, and while I did eventually cut my hair above my bra line, it was below my shoulders into my forties. I was convinced that I would "look like a man" if I cut my hair off. Today my hair is cut in a super short pixie cut, and no one has ever accused me of looking like a man. While this is a harmless example, it perfectly illustrates how often we are unaware that our Hard No's are not our own.

Thought Exercise:

Think of some Hard No's you have in your personal life. What is...

1. Something you absolutely will not do? Why?

   _____

   _____

   _____

   _____

   _____

2. Somewhere you absolutely will not go to? Why?

   _____

   _____

   _____

   _____

   _____

3. Someone you will absolutely not interact with? Why?

   _____

   _____

   _____

   _____

   _____

4. Something you would never buy? Why?

_____

_____

_____

_____

_____

5. Something you absolutely would not allow in your home? Why?

_____

_____

_____

_____

_____

As women, we often absorb the Hard No's of society and others as our own without realizing it. We aren't encouraged as little girls to think through and feel out our own personal boundaries, and we are taught to respect others' boundaries as more important than our own. Many religions teach that women are lesser beings than men – whether that is explicitly stated or not – and many cultures are based on patriarchal practices and power structures. We are socialized beginning in toddlerhood to behave within specific gender norms and to align ourselves with our culture's current fantasy of what being a female should look like.

The opposite side of the coin is the "Oh, Heck Yes." Our Oh, Heck Yes's are largely dictated to us by outside forces, just as our Hard No's are. Female presenting humans are socialized to adhere to certain behavioral standards and to be responsible for certain tasks. For instance, the phrase "women's work" is used to describe a task that is generally considered to be something that men should not have to do. Not only should a man not have to do said task, but a woman should *want* to do it (in other words, it should be a Heck Yes); and a woman should not want to do those tasks that are generally considered to be masculine in nature (a Hard No). This underlying cultural belief impacts everything from the division of household labor to the division of workforce labor.

Thought Exercise:

List ten things that are Oh, Heck Yes's for you. These can be spiritual, cultural, behavioral, etc.

Often, our Oh, Heck Yes isn't so much of a vehement agreement as it is an acquiescence. It's easy to mistake a simple yes for an Oh, Heck Yes if you have not considered where the belief came from. Any belief that is religious or cultural in origin should be examined carefully, as should concepts that you were taught in childhood. There isn't anything intrinsically wrong with a plain Yes, but your goal should be to own each and every one of your beliefs. As you explore your plain Yes's you may very well find that some of them are actually a "Should" and not an "Oh, Heck Yes."

"Don't 'should' on yourself."
– Jen Pastiloff

"Should" and "Supposed To" frequently masquerade as Heck Yes's that become buried in our psyche. Statements that start with "I should…" or include the phrase "…are supposed to…" are clear indicators that what you are talking about is not a Heck Yes for you. "Shoulds" become the standard by which we measure ourselves: we *should* have a cleaner house, we *should* be nicer, we *should* have more money in the bank, we *should* be thinner, we *should* be married by now, we *should* have children by now – the list of Shoulds never ends.

Thought Exercise:

List three Heck Yes concepts, behaviors, or boundaries that you feel strongly about. For each one, consider the following questions:

1. Is this a Should or is it a Heck Yes?

2. Is this my own idea and conviction? If not, where do you think it originated from? Hint: If it includes any form of the word "should" or the phrase "supposed to," it originated from an outside source.

_____

_____

_____

_____

_____

3. Does it benefit me? If so, how? If not, who does it benefit?

_____

_____

_____

_____

_____

◇◇◇◇

Thought Exercise:

1. What is the worst job you have ever had? Using the concept of mindfulness, consider the job you've chosen, and answer the following questions:
   A. What were the three things that stand out in your mind as the worst qualities of this job? The three best?

_____
_____
_____
_____
_____

B.   Describe a specific incident that hap-
     pened or a specific memory that you
     have of this job. Who was there? What
     was the setting or environment of that
     incident? What immediate effect did
     that incident have on you?

_____
_____
_____
_____
_____
_____
_____
_____
_____

C.   In what ways has that job influenced
     your life positively since then? In what
     ways, if any, has that job influenced
     your life negatively?

_____
_____
_____
_____

_____

_____

_____

_____

_____

_____

D. If you were able to go back in time, how would you change your role/behavior/ contribution to this job? In hindsight, what, if anything, could you have done that would have improved your experience?

_____

_____

_____

_____

_____

_____

_____

_____

_____

E. List three reasons why you are thankful for that job.

_____

_____

_____

2. Think of the most unpleasant coworker that you have ever worked with. Using the concept

of mindfulness, consider the coworker you've chosen, and answer the following questions:

A. What are three reasons why you found this person to be unpleasant?

_____

_____

_____

_____

_____

B. Describe a specific memory that you have of this coworker. Were you alone or in a group? Was exactly did they do that makes this memory stand out?

_____

_____

_____

_____

_____

_____

_____

_____

_____

C. Does it still upset you to think about this coworker now? If yes, why do you think that is? If no, why do you think it doesn't?

_____

_____

_____

_____

_____

_____

_____

_____

_____

_____

D. What was the immediate effect that their behavior had on your life? Long term?

_____

_____

_____

_____

_____

_____

_____

_____

E. List three reasons why you are thankful that you had the experience of working with this person.

_____

_____

_____

_____

_____

_____

_____

_____

_____

3. Thinking back over all of your past positions, is there one negative thing or quality that they all have in common?

_____

_____

_____

_____

_____

A. Is this quality indicative of an interpersonal theme, an environmental theme, or a task related theme? Is it a combination?

_____

_____

_____

_____

_____

B. Is this theme reflected in your personal life? If so, how? If not, why do you think that is?

_____

_____

_____

_____

_____

C. Do you see this as being something you have any control over? Why or why not?

_____

_____

_____

_____

_____

D. List three action items you can do to avoid having this theme repeat itself in your next position.

_____

_____

_____

_____

_____

E. List three internal/personal changes you can make to avoid this theme repeating itself in your next position.

_____

_____

_____

_____

_____

_____

_____

_____

_____

4. What culture have you least enjoyed working or living alongside or amongst? This can be a foreign culture altogether or a subculture of your own locale. Without judgement or censorship of yourself, consider the following questions:

A. What is it about this particular culture that bothers you? List as many specific qualities, behaviors, traditions, etc. as come to mind.

_____

_____

_____

_____

_____

_____

_____

_____

_____

_____

B. Think of one specific negative interaction with/incident involving this culture that stands out in your memory. What bothered you the most about it? Why did it bother you so much?

_____

_____

_____

_____

_____

_____

_____

_____

_____

C. List the three strongest emotions you feel now when you think back over this incident. Are they the same emotions you felt during the incident? How are they the same or different?

_____

_____

_____

_____

_____

_____

_____

_____

D. How have your feelings about this culture changed over time? Do they impact your behavior today?

_____

_____

_____

_____

_____

_____

_____

_____

_____

5. Consider your spiritual beliefs. What are
   three spiritual Hard No's for you?

_____

_____

_____

_____

_____

A. How did you come to have these beliefs
   – were they taught to you, or did you
   develop them on your own? When?

_____

_____

_____

_____

_____

_____

_____

_____

_____

B. Do you share these beliefs with a greater
   community? With your friends? With
   your significant other?

_____

_____

_____

_____

_____

_____

_____

_____

_____

C. How do these beliefs affect your everyday
   life? Do they affect the schedule of your
   day? Do they affect who you hang out with?

_____

_____

_____

_____

_____

_____

_____

_____

D. How "hard" are these no's for you? Are
   they Hard No's because you have chosen
   them yourself or have they been chosen
   for you as part of a larger spiritual
   tradition? How do you feel about that?

_____

_____

_____

_____

_____

_____

_____

_____

_____

_____

Bonus Exercise: The term "Hard No" is commonly used to refer to a sexual act that you absolutely will not do. Think of one of your sexual Hard No's. Why is it a Hard No for you? Did you decide it's a Hard No after experiencing it or is it based on a belief? How has this affected your life (sexually or otherwise)? Now think of a sexual act that used to be a Hard No for you, but is no longer one. What happened that changed your mind? How has changing your mind on that Hard No affected your life?

_____

_____

_____

_____

_____

_____

_____

_____

_____

Chapter 8:

Understanding

You're almost there! Step "U" is for Understanding. This step takes all of the information that you have gathered about yourself in steps E, I, and O and integrates them for you into a clear sense of self. I'm so excited for you to meet yourself!

> *"It's no use going back to yesterday, because*
> *I was a different person then."*
> **– Lewis Carroll**

You are a different person than you were five weeks ago, five months ago, five years ago...the challenge is to understand who we are at any given moment. Knowing yourself intimately gives you the information you need to make decisions that bring you joy, decisions that benefit you, and decisions that fuel your growth. This step is the culmination of the three prior steps; this is where the puzzle pieces come together to form a complete image.

Thought Exercise:
Review Results of Steps E, I, and O

Review the results of the thought exercises in each step below. Make a list of five things that you learned about yourself in when doing each one, following the directions below. These answers may come directly from the results of the thought exercises or they can be things you learn while reviewing your answers. If you want to redo one or all of those exercises, feel free! You are becoming acquainted with the you that you have become over the years, and you are worth digging deep for.

Five things from Step E – External Preferences: List five things that you learned about your External Preferences while working through this step.

_____

_____

_____

_____

_____

_____

_____

_____

_____

_____

Five things from Step I – Internal Truths: List five Internal Truths that you learned about yourself that you were previously unaware of.

_____

_____

_____

_____

_____

_____

_____

_____

_____

_____

_____

Five things from Step O – Oh, Heck No/Oh, Heck Yes: For this exercise, list five things that are "Oh, Heck Yes!" for you.

_____

_____

_____

_____

_____

_____

_____

_____

_____

_____

_____

*"Once a woman has done the work of
remembering herself, she is much more able to
change the world effectively."*
– Vicki Noble

Perhaps you don't feel like you've changed that much from your "before kids" days. Or maybe, like me, you barely recognize yourself now when you look back. Either way, having a clear understanding of who you were and what made you tick before you raised your kids will better help you to understand who you have become. The following exercise is meant to delineate the differences between who you were before you had children and who you are now.

Thought Exercise:
Before and After Chart

You'll need paper and a pencil for this exercise. Take the piece of paper and either fold it into fourths or draw four columns. Fill in the first column with this list, one concept per row:

Occupation

Hobby

Political affiliation

Spiritual practice

Night owl/Early bird

Favorite holiday

Overall health

Sexual Orientation

Dream/lifetime goal

Now label the second column "Before Kids," the third column "After Kids," and the fourth column "Notes."

Now, consider the concepts listed from the standpoint of before and after you were a parent. Jot down a few notes in the Before Kids column for each concept. Has anything changed over time? If so, use the After Kids column to make a few notes indicating what has changed for you. If nothing has changed, use the Notes column to indicate whether or not you have explored this area for yourself recently. If you have not thought about that concept anytime recently, take this opportunity to meditate on it.

_____

_____

_____

_____

_____

_____

_____

_____

_____

_____

_____

_____

_____

_____

_____

_____

_____

_____

_____

_____

_____

_____

Bonus Exercise: Create a second chart. This time, list five to ten concepts that you know *have* changed for you since you became a parent. They can be beliefs, likes or dislikes, physical attributes, desires, etc. Complete the Before Kids and After Kids columns just as you did before, but this time, use the Notes column to note what inspired that change. Was the change inspired by someone you met? Was the change in response to an event or incident? How has this change affected your life? Do you like yourself better now? Why or why not? Use this chart as an opportunity to reflect on the growth you have experienced while raising your children and to appreciate the person that you have become. Well done! _____

_____

_____

_____

_____

_____

_____

_____

_____

_____

_____

❖❖❖

Thought Exercise:
Make a Should List

Plan to start this exercise at the beginning of your day, but you'll want to finish it that same day. You'll need something to jot down some notes on throughout your day, whether you like to use good old fashion paper and pencil, or type notes into your tablet or phone, or you can even text yourself to keep track. As you move through your day, pay careful attention to the words you use in conversation, and also to your thoughts. Make a note of the times you used or thought the word "should" in regards to yourself (I *should* have done this, I *should* do that, etc.). At the end of the day, consider each item on your Should List: this time, change each one to either an Oh, Heck No! or an Oh, Heck Yes! Notice how many times during the day that you Should all over yourself. Is there a theme to your Should List? Do you see a recurring pattern? How can you be more authentic to yourself in the future?

_____

_____

_____

_____

_____

_____

_____

_____

_____

"Where there is no vision, the people perish."
– Proverbs 29:18

People want nothing more than to be seen. We want to be seen and acknowledged for who we are at our core. We are going to take this concept literally and create a tangible representation of who you are so that you will have a visual reminder going forward.

A vision board is nothing more than a collection of images and quotes mounted on the flat surface of your choice. I have two favorite types of vision boards and they both serve different purposes. The first is the traditional vision board, which is usually printed images and quotes glued, taped or stapled to sturdy paper. This type of vision board is generally static: it captures a specific idea or concept for one to focus on. This is most usually done using a poster board, which can be found at most drugstores, grocery stores, and office supply stores for under five dollars. You could also use card stock, the blank backside of a roll of wrapping paper or you can just tape or staple together several pieces of whatever kind of paper you have lying around the house. This isn't an art project, and you're not going to be graded, so use whatever makes sense for your budget. Everyone's budget loves free things, so get creative: just cut apart an old cardboard box if you've got one!

The second type of vision board would be a surface that you can reuse. A corkboard and tacks work well for this, as does a chalkboard or whiteboard and tape. Little did you know that your refrigerator was the perfect surface to use as a reusable vision board! You could even take thumbtacks and use one of your interior walls if you wanted to, but just mind the tiny little holes.

◇◇◇◇

Thought Exercise:
Vision Board

For this exercise you can use either a reusable or static surface. Cut images and quotes out of magazines or print them off of the internet that represent *who you are now* and affix them to your vision board. This vision board represents you and only you: there should be no pictures of your kids, spouse or pets on it. Use as many images and quotes as you need to build an accurate visual representation of who you are as an individual. This vision board is not meant to be used for manifesting goals or dreams, but instead it is meant to be a collection of images that embody who you have become.

The images you choose should represent some of your External Preferences, some of your Internal Truths and some of your Oh, Heck Yes's. Since we are becoming acquainted with who we have become as opposed to who we are not, only use images that are positive in nature. For example, an image of a positive External Preference might show the beach, the desert or a fire in a fireplace if you love being warm. An image of a positive Internal Truth might be one that represents your current spiritual practice. An image of a positive Oh, Heck Yes might be that of a political concept that you are passionate about. The point of the vision board is to accurately portray who you *are* as opposed to who you are *not*.

_____

_____

_____

_____

_____

_____

_____

_____

_____

_____

_____

Bonus Exercise: Share your vision board with at least two people who know you well and trust. If you have a spouse or partner, they should be one of the two people. Tell them what each item on the board represents in your life and explain what meaning it has to you. Ask them for feedback: which items on there were a surprise to them? Which items on the board don't feel authentic to them, and why or why not? This is a good opportunity to glean insight from them – do they see other changes in you that you've overlooked? Just be careful to choose two people who you trust to have your best interests at heart so that the feedback you get is genuine and caring.

- -

- -

_____

_____

_____

_____

_____

_____

_____

_____

_____

_____

CHAPTER 9

You Are Always the Answer!

This is what you've been working towards: figuring out what to do with your life. This step of the process will show you how to create a goal for the next stage of your life built specifically out of what you now know about yourself.

> *"I am the gate keeper of my own destiny: I will have my glory day in the hot sun."*
> **– Ignacio, Nacho Libre**

You've completed Step A (Assess the Situation), where you sat down and made a thoughtful and objective compilation of your assets and current situation. You've completed Step E (External

Preferences) where you've explored how your tastes have changed. You've completed Step I (Internal Truths) and have taken a closer look at your beliefs and values. You've finished Step O (Oh, Heck No/ Oh, Heck Yes) where you explored the difference between a Should and an Oh, Heck No and an Oh, Heck Yes so that you can be more authentic to yourself. Then you took all of that and integrated it into a clearer understanding of who you have become in Step U (Understanding).

Step Y contains the answer to the question that inspired you to buy this book. The letter Y stands for "You," as in "*You* are always the answer!" You are *always* the answer to the question. You can't know what you want to do with your life if you don't know what makes you tick.

Think about your life as a mother. How did you help your children solve problems of this nature? You started out with questions like, "What do you like to do?" and "What interests you?" and "What makes you happy?" and "What gives your life purpose?" The difference between you and your children is that your children actually knew the answers to those questions. Their personal obligations and the needs of those around them hadn't sucked the life out of them yet. They were still able to access the parts of themselves needed to make goals for their lives.

You are always the answer. What do I mean by that? I mean that you have not been able to decide what you want to do with your life because you no longer knew what brings you happiness, what you find value in, what gives your life purpose, and what you feel strongly about. Additionally, you were no longer aware of your Hard No's and your Hard Yes's. The Hard No's function like the rumble strips on the side of the highway: if you find yourself on the rumble strips, you'll know that you've strayed too far from the center of your road. Your Hard Yes's help you to more easily narrow down your destination. You now have the skills it takes to learn more about yourself whenever you need to. And, frankly, a day doesn't go by where I don't have to do more self-discovery.

Thought Exercise:
A/E/I/O/Understanding chart

You'll need paper (lined paper or graph paper work best, just for visual clarity) and pencil for this exercise. Take your paper and divide it into five columns, labeled A – Assess, E – External, I – Internal, O – Oh, Heck Yes, and lastly, O – Oh, Heck No. Look back over the thought exercises that you worked through in chapters four through seven, and review any notes or journal entries you may have made. As you do, write words and short phrases in the appropriate columns. Specifically, use words or concepts that relate to the reason you bought this book: to figure out what to do with your life after your kids are grown. Try to list as many words/concepts in each column as possible. Try to complete this chart using only words or phrases that are authentic to you.

In the future, you can complete this chart geared towards any issue that you are trying to solve. Visual charts such as this are really helpful when trying to get clarity on issues that feel muddy or to work through issues that affect more than one person. For instance, if you and your spouse are struggling to decide between downsizing to a smaller home or remodeling the one that you have now that the kids are gone, completing this chart with input from both of you will help you to better understand the other and come to an agreement.

_____

_____

_____

_____

_____

_____

_____

_____

_____

_____

_____

_____

_____

_____

_____

_____

_____

_____

_____

_____

_____

Bonus exercise: review your chart with your significant other and your closest friend. If you don't have a significant other, consider sharing it with another close friend. Be sure to choose people to share this with that know you well and care for you – this isn't the time to ask an estranged relative for their input. Ask them where they agree or disagree based on their knowledge of you *now*. Ask them what they would add to the chart that isn't there. If they've known you for a long time, ask them if they see any items that have changed since you first met. Why do they think that item is different now? Why do *you* think it has changed?

_____

_____

_____

_____

_____

_____

_____

_____

_____

_____

_____

A/E/I/O/U Format

This is where you will take all of the information that you've learned about yourself and use it to answer the question that led you to pick this book up in the first place. The A/E/I/O/U Format is simply a way to frame the issue in a clear and concise manner that reflects the Always Y process. Doing this allows you to include parameters that qualify the solution and eliminate unnecessary confusion.

An example of an issue stated in A/E/I/O/U Format would be, "I need a job that is fast paced where I can work with animals and have Sundays off."

I need *a job (A – Assess the Situation)* that is *fast paced (E – External Preferences)* where I can *work with animals (I – Internal Truths)* and have *Sundays off (O – Oh, Heck No!/Oh Heck Yes!)*.

Another example of a problem stated in A/E/I/O/U Format would be "I'm looking for a nursing job where I can work from home and still help others but that doesn't require me to go back to school."

I'm looking for a *nursing job (A – Assess the Situation)* where I can *work from home (E –*

External Preferences) while still *helping others (I – Internal Truths)* but that doesn't require me to go *back to school (O – Oh, Heck No/Oh, Heck Yes).*

While those two example sentences are cut and dried, you can always include additional E/I/O details to give yourself more information to work with. An example of this would be "I want a career with good benefits that allows me to have a flexible schedule where I can work with the elderly without having to work nights or weekends or do physical labor."

I want a *career (A – Assess the Situation)* with *good benefits (E – External Preferences)* that allows me to have a *flexible schedule (E – External Preferences)* where I can work *with the elderly (I – Internal Truths)* without having to *work nights or weekends (O – Oh, Heck No/Oh, Heck Yes)* or do *physical labor (O – Oh, Heck No/Oh, Heck Yes).*

Thought Exercise:
State the Problem in A/E/I/O/U Format

Using the chart you completed above, state the problem or goal in A/E/I/O/U Format five different ways. The problem may stay the same in each sentence, but be sure to use at least five different items for the I/O/U portions of the sentence.

_____

_____

_____

_____

_____

_____

_____

_____

_____

_____

_____

_____

_____

_____

_____

_____

_____

_____

_____

_____

_____

You Are *Always* the Answer

You really do have the answers to all of your questions inside of you. That's not just a cliché either. Consider a five-year-old child: when they have a decision to make, there is no confusion or hesitation. If you ask a five-year-old what they want to eat, they can tell you immediately. If you ask them what they want to watch on television, there is no hesitation whatsoever. This isn't because five-year-olds have some strange wisdom that we gradually lose over the years – it's because they are fully connected to themselves. Young children are very much in touch with their own likes, dislikes and goals because they have never needed to take anyone else's into account.

The reason why you have struggled so much with planning for your life after kids is because you simply didn't know yourself anymore. You truly did not have the tools necessary to make a decision that would have brought you joy and satisfaction – and not because there was anything wrong with you. You have spent many, many years helping your children to achieve their own individuation, very likely at the loss of your own. Using the Always Y process to rediscover yourself is a great place to start.

CHAPTER 10:

This Might Hurt a Little…

Here's the thing about personal growth: it can be really painful. Growth demands change, whether it be a change in behavior or a change in thought processes. Implementing that change can be very painful.

I'm the type of person who falls down proverbial rabbit holes of thought, Alice in Wonderland style. Every positive change in my life has been the result of hundreds of hours of study, deep reflection and painful realizations. I read books, blogs, articles, and scientific journals. I watch lectures, videos, TED Talks, documentaries, seminars, and vlogs. I listen to podcasts, audiobooks, and lectures. I love retreats and seminars, and I'm a member of a myriad of Facebook groups and online communities.

This book is the current culmination of my own painful struggle for growth. Instead of developing a strong sense of self during my childhood and adolescent years, I developed the ability to adapt and adjust in order to survive. This dubious skillset came in handy while I was raising my kids because my own wants and needs never conflicted with theirs. There was never a time when I really struggled with giving up what I wanted in order to please my kids, almost entirely due to my abject lack of wants and needs. I was so out of touch with myself as an individual separate from my kids that there was very little conflict. My marriage was also much easier to navigate because I simply mirrored my husband's needs and desires.

It wasn't until I experienced breast cancer that I began to have needs that trumped my children's or my husband's. It wasn't until I was quite literally forced by the universe to take care of myself (or die!) that I started to recognize my own needs and to take care of myself. Those first needs were baby steps, but they set me down the path of re-individuation. I won't lie to you – it was *hard!* It still *is* hard! Having spent the first thirty-seven years of my life putting the needs of others before my own absolutely numbed me to what needs I may have had. Even my chosen profession demanded that I be self-sacrificing. My entire life was built around being as need-less as was humanly possible.

Once I started honoring my needs, though, the floodgates slowly creaked open, and I began to entertain the concept of actually honoring my own wants, too. Remember those jagged Frankenstein scars across my back? They are precious to me now. Every time I saw my back in the mirror, every time that I got out of our shower (it was directly across from the mirror in our bathroom), every time that I had to wear a bathing suit, I was reminded of the horror of that experience. I hated my back. Strangely, I was able to give myself far more grace when looking in the mirror at my reconstructed breasts. And then one day I had the most glorious epiphany – I would change what I saw in the mirror everyday by getting a tattoo!

And so I did. Not just a small, pretty, feminine tattoo, either. I got an enormous back piece. I searched for exactly the right artist to design it for me, and we communicated via email about what I wanted. The tattoo is *perfect*. The experience was transformative: I took the thing that caused me such horrible emotional pain and turned it into the most beautiful part of my body in my own eyes. Now every day that I get in and out of the shower or go to the pool, all I see is the beauty of the beautiful image on my back.

I hear you asking, "How does that count as individuation? What does that have to do with anything?" Little did I know that it has *everything* to do with individuation.

We were still actively attending an evangelical Christian church at the time, and tattoos were sternly frowned upon. Sure, no one would say anything if you got a Bible verse tattooed on you, but that's not what I did. Neither my husband nor I had any tattoos at that point in our life, either, which made me the first to do so. His family was (and perhaps still is) vehemently opposed to tattoos. They even have Bible verses memorized to back up their horror and indignation. Additionally, my own husband didn't really like tattoos in general, much less did he think that giant ones on women were ever a good thing. Any of my female friends that had tattoos had small ones that they were embarrassed of and hid as much as possible.

But my need to not feel the daily pain of seeing the scars on my back was stronger than my need to remain small and unseen. That impetus propelled me forward despite the almost palpable disapproval of those closest to me. It quite literally took my husband – the man who without a doubt loves me for who I am and encourages me every day to be myself without fear – six months to like my back piece. Six. Months. Six months of him being very supportive of me doing what I needed to do to feel better while I was very much aware that he didn't want to look at or talk about the tattoo. I was actually less physically attractive in his eyes after the addition of the tattoo. But *I loved it.*

I loved everything about it: the design, the color choices, the placement, and what each part of the design signified to me. Even more than that, though, I loved the newfound feeling of ownership of my own life. For the first time in the thirty-eight years I had spent on Earth, I felt like I had known what I wanted to do, and I had *done* it, regardless of what other people wanted. That is the very definition of individuation, and my journey of self-discovery had begun.

My beautiful friend, the astrologer and psychotherapist Eugenia Krok, would tell you that only by knowing yourself fully can you live a more fulfilled life. I believe that the reason I'm as healthy and functional of a human being as I am today is because of my insatiable quest for knowledge. The problem with that quest for knowledge, however, is that once you have it, you have to choose what you are going to do with it. This is where you, dear reader, find yourself now.

You now understand the Always Y process. You've used it to give you the tools to figure out what you're going to do with your life once your kids have flown the coop. Hopefully you've worked through this book with an open heart and a genuine desire to better learn who you have become while you were raising your children. Now you find yourself a crossroads:

will mindfulness, self-reflection, and inquiry become part of who you are? Will the desire to know yourself deeper and to show up more authentically for yourself in your life remain, or will you rejoin the Stepford-ization of American women? The choice is yours.

I can't pretend that there aren't any risks involved. While my back piece was the beginning of my real life as my true self, it was also the beginning of the end of many other things. Over the eight years since my breast cancer diagnosis, I have made many, many life changing decisions on my path to re-individuation. My life barely resembles what it was like previously. Yet every decision I make that moves me closer to being my authentic true self costs something. In the words of my beloved girlfriend Kristi Sisemore: "Your journey to be healthier makes us all healthier, even though it's flipping annoying sometimes to have to constantly evaluate one's behavior and motivations."

The risks are both simple and difficult: every decision you make that is outside of the norm that you've previously worked within will put you at odds with someone. Your decision to have an opinion that differs from your partner's may be the cause of many arguments. Your decision to investigate parts of you that you perhaps never have before – such as your sexuality – may alienate your friends and family. Your decision to take a job that keeps you from being home in time to cook dinner every night may be inconvenient to those who now have to cook for themselves. Your decision to cut all your hair off because you've always wanted to and never have before may not go over well with your kids. You decision to explore other spiritual paths may cost you friendships and sense of community.

However, the risks of *not* unearthing your true authentic self are far worse. Your house is about to be empty of your children: that will leave just you, and if you have one, your spouse or partner. What will you talk about? What will you do to fill your days? How will you stay alive? If you choose the path of least resistance now, you are choosing to die. You will be choosing to slowly die over the next twenty years (or less, if you're lucky). There's only so much vacuuming and grocery shopping one can do for a household of two.

Don't live out the rest of your life as nothing more than a human placeholder. Come alive. Discover the adventure that is you, and live life to the fullest!

> *"A life without passion is a slow way*
> *to freeze to death."*
> **– Anonymous**

CHAPTER 11:

This Is Not the End

"Change is inevitable; growth is optional."
– Anonymous

American women are taught from the cradle to be an ideal and not an individual. We are indoctrinated with social, cultural and religious concepts of acceptable femaleness starting in toddlerhood. The first third of our life is spent absorbing these constructs and conforming to them: wear pink (or yellow or light green, if you must); keep your legs crossed (don't show your panties!); be gentle in comparison to your male counterparts; don't be loud; don't be sports-centered; be good at reading and writing; be good with animals and children; be able to cook (and enjoy doing it!); be virtuous (whatever that means!); remain a virgin until after your wedding vows; and always, always, always be willing to put yourself last. Nowhere in there are we encouraged to be an individual. No one encourages young girls to go, do, and learn – unless it's within the designated norms.

We spend the second third of our life in service to our families. This Stepford-ization of American femininity does well for us while raising our kids, yet it leaves us completely lost once they have grown up. But life happens: our kids grow up and leave home, leaving us alone with our thoughts and without purpose. Illness and injury happen, forcing us to change careers, or depriving us of the opportunity to achieve the goals we had previously set.

The change in American culture over the last fifty years has meant that there have been no women to look to as role models for our experience becoming empty-nesters. We are the first generation of women to work full-time both in and out of the home while still getting our kids to soccer practices and dance classes, still reading fifteen minutes per night with each child and feeding them healthy organic meals. We, the American women, have had no time to do anything other than stay in our mommy lane.

Then, suddenly, the empty nest looms ahead of us, and we have some big decisions in front of us – decisions that frankly, we are not prepared to make. We have perfected the art of service to others and we have forgotten how to hear our own voice or see our own needs. We have no firm sense of identity and we have no idea how to find one. Every facet of the media carefully dictates what we should look like, what cars we should drive and what kind of jewelry we should want to wear. Every detail of our life is homogenized for us, even down to the type of exercise we should be doing this year.

The Always Y process gives us the tools to undo the damage done by our culture. It gives us the ability to get reacquainted with ourselves at our core, which gives us tools needed to plan a future that we can enjoy. Self-awareness is integral to making sound decisions, and this process is a roadmap to self-awareness and individuation.

"Everything has changed and yet,
I am more me than I've ever been."
– Iain Thomas

ACKNOWLEDGMENTS

First, foremost, and most importantly, my deepest gratitude goes to my husband Jim. I am who I am today because you have always believed in me. Your love for me through the years has been the very breath in my lungs and the blood in my veins. This book exists only because of you. I adore you.

To my amazing kids, Norah and Smith – thank you. From the bottom of my heart, thank you. You guys have been my inspiration to grow and heal since the very moment that I learned of your existence. You've brought more joy and laughter into my life than I ever imagined possible. You are my greatest achievements, and I am insanely proud of you both.

Thank you to my beautiful sisters for your unwavering support as I tossed the dirty laundry out there for all to see. I love you.

Many, many thanks to my Author Incubator family. Thank you especially to Dr. Angela Lauria, CEO & Founder of The Author Incubator, for inspiring me to get out of my comfort zone and for sharing your vision with me when I couldn't see a dang thing. Thank you to my Developmental Editor, Ora North, for your kindness and encouragement, and to my Managing Editor, Moriah Howell, for being such a supportive partner in the process when I was struggling. Many more thanks to everyone else at TAI, specifically Ramses Rodriguez for keeping me sane (not the easiest task!), and Cheyenne Giesecke for having the answers to all of my many, many questions – with a smile.

Thank you to David Hancock and the Morgan James Publishing team for helping me bring this book to print and this dream to life.

Thank you to the inimitable Amy Ferris, my SHEro. Your fiery words and gracious friendship have deeply impacted my life, and your fierce championing of woman-kind inspires me to use my own voice more bravely every single day. Thank you to Jen Pastiloff for helping me to see that yes, even *I* am "fallinloveable", and for teaching me not to Should on myself. Thank you to my #kripsisters for sharing your strength and love with me when I needed it most.

Lastly, to my chosen family and my tribe – y'all know who you are - thank you for loving me, for cheering me on, and for not abandoning ship when I was holed up writing this book. Your overwhelming support and non-stop encouragement during this process quite literally sustained me. Thank you.

And yes, Ethan, the moon *is* a hologram.

Thank You!

Thank you so much for using this book as part of your journey of self-re-discovery. I know firsthand just how difficult this process can be, especially if you've experienced trauma or abuse. I also know that the process can feel very lonely if you don't have the support of a strong, feminine community alongside you.

I'd like to invite you to join the Meaning After Momming – Beyond the Empty Nest Facebook group: https://www.facebook.com/groups/595520210940573/? ref=share.

In it, you'll be able to interact with other women on the path of re-individuation, have access to an ever-growing list of resources for growth, find more thought exercises, and connect with me personally. Join me and the amazing women of the Meaning After Momming – Beyond the Empty Nest tribe for a cup of coffee or a glass of wine wherever you are, and welcome to the Tribe!

About the Author

Amie Eyre Newhouse is a registered nurse and writer from the Hill Country of Austin, Texas. She draws on her twenty-four-plus years as a nurse along with her own personal experience as a breast cancer survivor and a survivor of childhood trauma as she champions other women on their own journeys of self-discovery. With a hard-earned understanding the fragility of life from both sides of the bed rail, Amie is passionate about truth, authenticity, and intentional living. Having always been a little left of center, Amie first began incorporating the practices of mindfulness, visualization, and meditation as pain management tools into her nursing while caring for palliative and hospice patients almost twenty years ago. These days, you can usually find Amie on her back deck with her mostly-adult kids, husband, friends, and dogs, deep in discussion about social justice issues and human rights or fervently planning the demise of the patriarchy.

CPSIA information can be obtained
at www.ICGtesting.com
Printed in the USA
JSHW032306040820
7114JS00003B/110